Talking Crow

Spiderwize
Remus House
Coltsfoot Drive
Woodston
Peterborough
PE2 9BF

www.spiderwize.com

Edited by James Clarkson
Photography by James Clarkson, Norman Clarkson, Polly Clarkson, David Brown and
James Clarkson.
Cover and layout by Camilla Davis

TALKING CROW

CONTENTS

FROM THE COUNTRY

Fort strong,
his hedge grows in deep rectangles;
in concrete casement squares
tied down to a wind-proofed inner tree-line.

He has seen it all.
Cow shit, warble fly, afterbirth, barn fire.
Cancer and haemorrhage; canker and blight.
Infestation after infestation.

He has seen from here the death of his boss;
followed by that of his boss' daughter.
He has heard murder. He has marauded. He has braved a bog
for a long-crashed bomber's block of aiming glass.

Tonight has brought quiet and he paces with the bin.
It is grass-quiet. He is grass-quiet.
So, stepping quietly, he crosses the lawn
to chain up his great iron roller.

Steam builds around the lit-up house.
He patrols it, pausing only
to circle a plant wedged into a thick-edged sink planter
sat at an angle on a steel drain lid.

That abyss is secure now,
but he has spent many days down there, unblocking.
And each time he came back up, he came back up from a world reeking
into a world reeking.

He walks the borders one final time.
From his Tree of Heaven he senses some heavy blackbird turf-chatter.
From beyond his hedge, he hears the unstill fields sweep and crack
with the shifting of the soil and the wind's lazy smack.

HALLELUJAH HERE

A place of snapped pavements and small victories;
of things cobbled;
of nothing coming together.

A falling into the sun place,
a place where spirits and long-removed fence posts
have more substance than what actually exists.

I think these things coming back from the shop
bringing breakfast milk.

I will forget the better part of them.
Or if I remember them,
then I will think only about their failure as words;
as word disease.

Such is the hallelujah place;
this place of searching.

So search in the most profound deep
if you want even the smallest signal in the dark -
use the most sensitive instruments.

Search and search.
Search and still there will be nothing.
But at least *that* door will be closed.

THINGS TO COME

Voodoo maraca-shook beat of an indicator
ticks in time with a nodding line of trees
that wind noosed by a loop of train track.

The rest of my car whines along too, as a spider hangs
between wing-mirror and wet driver's-side door.
Tiny, soused, demon-black hobo-traveller
moving with what I endow it; its web
a useless, oily, return-entry chute
bobbling on a false flow of air.

On the passenger seat there's a bag stuffed with Chinese food:
Chicken balls; spittle-thick sweet-and-sour;
my half-arsed conscience food of tofu in satay sauce.

Each concoction
fumes in its plastic box,
gassing the windows with an exotic stench.
As the engine vibrates,
spiced shaky droplets descend
in bomb-runs to damp-blast the rubber seals.

With a hard lock left I am left facing an old person's home
where I see them behind glass, suffering
the reverse exorcism

of pig's-blood-thick children's voices
long after the little turds should have gone.
Lord knows why it is that they must bear them,
showing off how they
will continue to exist when
these trapped shakers have passed on.

Luckily I can blot their misery out with Our Jimi.
If I don't meet you no more in this world... Will I? Will I?
I'll meet you all on the next one...

...and don't be late. Don't be late!
Beautifully put.
So I leave that universe and get stuck into the next one
at a set of traffic lights
where middle-aged people
hum hate from their exhausts.

Our lives probably are about recurrence.
Which is depressing
when the car lopes into its ninth pothole.

The same fate again and again. No rest and no ending.
Horny little animals, snatching at scraps; living and suffering and passing.
Unbearable. But then again...
just think of the Sahara and think of vastnesses.
Just think of the wasted girdle of stars
spread wherever you look.

NEW YEAR'S DAY

I
Morning, coming to under clouds
rolling above some old shops.

From the house, marijuana fumes
gently pummel the pavement, spilling its guts
into v-shaped ruts that create signs on its surface.

There's a dead bird at a line
where the verge and path meet:
tarmac black and grass green are held by long thin wing bones;
head and beak bleached and bacteria-clean.

You move through this easily
knowing the shifts in pressure between hedges;
the bulge and tilt of the paths.

Above, Jupiter's solo struck-match brightness.
The year is heralded by a distant storm.

II
Still living birds glow in the wind,
cantilevered shapes against strips of sky.
Two giant leylandii mesh loudly,
their threshing trunks suggestively spread.
They are an entryway to a dingy, backwoods kingdom
of golf balls and high teenagers.
By a busy newsagents, two younger children giggle,
pushing their way in for fags or chocolate.
An older woman leaves, pelvis like a double-edged axe,
coughing up whatever toked battle-toxins she'd just ingested.
There was another cough from inside the shop too,
masculine, but lighter, like a eunuch.

III

Now the day progresses
with just enough light produced
to fuel your carnivorous visions of the street.

Odds and ends of wood spike in a bin;
houses are smothered in strings of outdoor bulbs;
a bundled national flag rags in a bare cherry tree,
its white and crabby red flashing.
It had been nailed to a plank, but was freed by the wind,
cartwheeling until it was caught in the claws of a branch.
Nails and wood, people and coughing, you and yours.
Souls pinned down by the effort
of being something for something else.

It's time to move on.
Light-weight quanta lift your view from nothing
to just a little more than nothing.

CLEARING THE HOUSE

Easily the wood snapped,
its strength cracked
down to ribs
or single broken strips.

Armfuls from the house
fell apart, use
becoming myth
at the tip mouth.

A fire saved more journeys –
ash dug under strawberries
could have been a van load,
but was simply reduced.

And what an offering was burned!
'History of England – Fully Illustrated',
covered by chipboard
and soon sent skyward.

Only car parts remained, filling
with water and resting on a flag
of sunken coal-hatch concrete;
its fire-breath stopped by dirt.

AT A FLEMISH RELIQUARY

Oaths and admiration enter
this vacuum of silver and bone;
a mined hand suggesting pause;
devout, pig-farmed fingers
prospecting for signs in the smoke.

Ideas change. Coups come and go.
Those who crept close to this fizzing ore
fist their freedom as they fist their dollars.

Elegant still, the silver holds,
unable to pilot or police;
glass grey, jewellery taken, bones gone;
its kept skin ragged clean;
its finger weight worked free.

PEAR CORE

Perfect double-bridge-curving core
heavy on the table;
a shadow and its object
both intent on having weight.

This equality of form,
driven electrically by a lamp,
exudes mass and pulses with movement.
It is insistent on pushing the full universe my way.

Then the pulled pin stalk
lying more heavy, more dense;
a thick truncheon beating the tame table wood;
a cylinder head cracked.

Drenched bulb of life, now ended.
Branch centre, enacting and reacting to my eyes.
Brilliant pale-gold god, prodding around.
Burst end.

Return now to the one place there is
where no acting is necessary.
Where agency, volition and choice
seep down into the winged background.

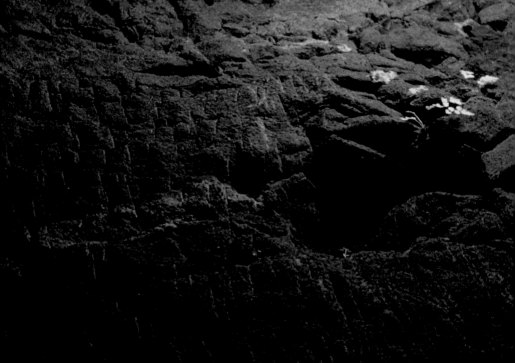

SINGING TO THE GODS

We trip over naughty sand
devising its curves as we go,
summoning gulls and
roping up worm casts too.

We put helicopters
and light planes into the sky;
we cool the waters
pooled in each waterway.

Then we stretch out the land,
humping it in places
with a purling hand and
smoothing it in others.

Later, we remodel the action
of the stars as the evening flows
through our fingers and on
beyond the night-deep windows.

LADY IN THE LABURNUM

Scissor-cut woman,
cutting back
at the golden chain's back-lit inflorescence
over long-chopped leaf litter.

How her hands claim the garden poison.

How she lops bursting bunches;
de-cultivating the murky,
danger-dirty,
green-topped bark.

My woman is a screamless grieving Demeter.

My woman is a soughing mistress, suggesting disaster
with a handful of chipped pea-pod pips.

Scissored and scalpelled,
thunder blights her bone.
Her smoke-blackened, lightning-layered
seams of skin groan.

She is totally undone.

I want to shout 'Just see it out lady, see it out –
the blue-lazered slice-lines will show the way.'

But this lady will rise not,
not even from a Cookham plot.

Not even from where
the heaviest heave of feathers are.

BORDER DISPUTE (For Bonnie)

It started in sunshine, with us tugging at a pair of shrubs
too well-set to be pulled up without terrible effort.
A deep clump of bamboo and a wisteria
were both slated for forced removal to a new site.

At first it was you alone, arse skyward,
digging around the edges, unsure of the task ahead;
unsure if one person could manage the bush-plucking
spade-job by themselves.

That's when I was lured;
your unfeathered reverse-role mating dance
getting me into some heavy forking
with your difficult green children.

As we began each plant adopted its ancient oppositional strategy
of clinging, pricking, curling and snagging.
Each used blades; each used splinters; each used dew-damp bud bullets.
Each had skin that barked our flesh.

In time we pushed through the Stalingrad of bamboo,
clearing out the leafy spear shoots at the base.
But the ground was still being held,
every clod fought for.

So we chopped in a frenzy,
cropping finally one core claw-root to deliver a listing, lifeless, emerald fang
that thirsted over its former gum-pit; an impotent totem
flopping at the mercy of the breeze.

The wisteria too was an unleashed Flagellant's whip;
a grappling hook, chucked onto the wood-preserved trellis.
Its fight was one of clever barbs designed to leave us Jesus-marked
as we stripped away its soil.

For that defiance we opened our torture box socket set,
persuading its blossoms with delicate skill to spill eventually out onto the
lawn.
Then our garden gangland pincers plied a trade of sap sapping,
letting it seep until, exhausted and minus several vascular fingers, it gave in.

The closing scene was one of D-Day devastation.
Mallets littered the dirt, AWOL leaves sheathed the grass.
Signature curlicues of branches lay scribbled over a war-lawn of battered
handles,
themselves lying log-jammed on the filthy earth plinth where we sat knack-
ered.

Onto this shroud we poured our sympathy at last,
wrapping the root-balls in gauze and offering water to the shattered tendrils.
We sacrificed time to coil cloth around any still-oozing tap roots;
two UN gardeners, tending to the wounded.

NIGHT OF THE MOTH

Maybe this miniature Mothman
could prophesise only the miniature
catastrophe of our car alarm going off
on a Sunday night.

Perhaps its curled antennae twitched
not because it saw our future
trapped in rubble or dead at a roadside,
but because it searched for a street light,
which it saw but couldn't reach
due to all the windows being closed.

It definitely reacted to being driven about,
appearing as a surprise twilight eye
in my rear view mirror as I tried to sort the electrics,
which we thought might have been upsetting the alarm.
It flapped and I flapped and I nearly drove
into a parked people carrier.

Happily, this didn't presage the roof being ripped off
or me being whisked off to a city in the clouds.
It led simply, as most phenomena do,
to a quiet release and a flight into the dusk.

A VIEWING

We step into your porch
Bristling from the cold void outside.

Straight away it's clear why you are selling - your wife is shaking.
It's barely noticeable,
But it happens along with a rumble in her lower lip.

Soon she will be making apologies for not coping,
But for now she makes the tea as you gently shuffle us around your home.

Five rooms are packed in close, dense with memories of drying hair;
Of eating breakfast on the edge of the bed;
Of homework and leftover-beef sandwiches on a Sunday.

These were rooms from a time when children and parents
Had nothing to say to each other.

Our chatty gaggle would gag in this silence.
They would also struggle with the smell of over-boiled veg.
Luckily your back garden offers a bit more hope.

Here there are fruit trees bent double
Over a row of raspberry bushes prepared for the winter.

There's an asbestos-panelled shed too, with a stock of dried seeds
Stored on a square of marbled newspaper reporting news from the 1990s.
It's out there we learn that you retired in 1986.

1986? In 1986 I was still at secondary school
While my wife was, well, still only allowed to write in pencil.

Thirty-odd years of escape has to have a handshake,
Although doing it feels out-of-date and you are out of practice;
So we give up half way through the third down-thrust.

I can't see my grip going through lack of use.
That deal was a good one back then,

Now it would be almost impossible unless you're the cautious type
Who puts a bit away and doesn't drink booze
Ever.

Back in the kitchen you show us a pantry
With shallow shelves stocked with tins.

There are plain biscuits and tea bags and pearl barley,
But no coffee and no olive oil.
In the fridge there would have been real butter and full fat milk.

After seeing your garage, which actually had a car in it, and a chat about your next home,
We leave being positive, but all four of us know we won't be back.

We return to the cold outside on your drive.
When you've gone there will be brown stains
On the tiled walls where your cupboards were.

WHAT WILL COME WHEN YELLOWSTONE BLOWS?

A tracked crane squats,
fenced in on the white stones
of a newly laid road.

Its bridge weight gropes up
urged on by the matchstick scramble
of fly-black, violin-tight wire
running from base to hook tip.

From ground level people stare
at the astonished metal
making deal after deal
with demanding, tantrum air.

This fashioned steeple arm defies
the trees, the birdless eaves
and the rocks waiting below.

MORNING AFTER THE ENGAGEMENT PARTY

I

We lie, emptied after a night on the various boozes;
after a night spent on the floor wrapped in a duvet.

Noise too broad-brimmed to be blocked by a door
filters upstairs in waves that break on beaten eardrums:

Bottles rattle into a bin; ceramic bowls clack; a hair drier starts up.
Outside a boy clatters content on a scooter, his wheels easing over rubble.

We lie, plugged into our crimson socket,
ear-bashed by the glad glass din of a house recovering.

II

In the garden our two boys have filled up a plastic pool and shriek as they leap,
feet slapping at the edge on sloshes of grass-fuelled waste water
voiding softly down into the soil.

We listen to the sound of a world on the turn.
There's a rumble from the train lines, a heavy diesel shudder.
The jumping has stopped; the lawn has become silent.

III

On the grass a vole has had its heart stopped.
Its felt-clinkered skull has become a red room for ants;
its puncture holes coned doors glittering under the kiss-sap of slugs;
its presence a torment for a dozen fuzzy cupids, desperate to inspect its end.

In time, tokens of blue,
grey and black party washing hang above the kill site.
Pretty, pegged-out vacant torso-forms,
sparkling sweetly as a shower approaches.

As we take down last night's tent,
we step carefully to avoid the soaked body-spot, returning later with spades.
But by then the velvet chunk was gone, probably being romanced by a cat's
bowels
or else sung to by the grub-litter of a nest writhing underfoot.

IV

We turn and the world turns: two capstan souls
loving and loved and lying, deft as reliquary skulls.
Ah, we kid ourselves about the weight of such things.
Look for love and there it is: one movement
amongst many; one simple moment of the spirit.

CHURCHYARD

Behind the church stand the saints in reverse;
hooked hands heavy with blessings,

lead beards scrolled,
glass robes shaped behind plastic.

Designed to sweeten light, their stained backs
gel with the mini-tombs of the newly cremated.

Slippy keys of stone, these are portal black
and almost just stone, but not quite.

Out here the wonders come densely packed.
The flight-path of birds tracked through bright yew space.

The gravel-pit pearls, layered under tubs of crystal-water.
The flowers, paradise-powdered and exposing their earthy scent.

And then there are the dead given to the ground; finger-ends bitten down;
numberless bone shambles, rambling loose in shut seams of wood.

SITE

Old sewer fence
not keeping anything in or out;
grey-brown apocalypse of form
sought by undergrowth,
caught in the flood of a wishing pool.

Pipe blocks, filling odd corners,
might as well be ancient ruins
part-looted for new buildings,
part-loved in a landscape
getting slippier by the day.

Worn blocked conduit
runs overhead from the bricked-up sewerage works
to a concrete manhole in an earth bank.
A wasps' nest once flickered there
making dog walkers risk barbed wire to avoid it.

Mounting a low rise to new houses,
my feet are laid on the brain-shaped
craze of tar spread cold on the path.
There is a wooden-walled alley
littered with a fresh chop of laurel.

Someone had lopped the top shoots
leaving them scattered.
Or they had been placed carefully
expecting a special entry
by someone secretly hovering.

Their toxins looked all but done
to be honest. Boots not bare feet
had squashed them sufficiently
so their still branched green tongues
lay all seeped out.

WINTER PROPELLER

Snow falls heavily,
divining the presence of an external house light.
It's an early swirling turbofan of cold
hissing out its cotton squeal.

My feet will soon combust in that cold.
I will soon wander in its coils.
I will also soon wonder at how such a chilly serpent
could leave a place so in need of the thread of an afterlife.

The air tires,
lifted and lost and dropped continuously;
a turbine edge brought down
to chop at inlets of spooling exhaust gas.

The bowels of this day lie
already spilled across a spoiled elevated altar;
its auguries, as always I'm afraid,
are looking unfavourable.

DRAINING SPADE

Through years of drain digging
your spade wore down until
fully half the blade disappeared.

On long days
you cut at the earth's top
shaping sharp foot-deep farm culverts.

Each section was a step-drained
dug-out length,
secured pipe piece by pipe piece.

During these digs
your spade got masking tape
where shaft met metal.

Navvies came for deep work
and you watched their bog-spades
slice out fourteen-foot pits.

And you watched their payment
spent on beer and slept off
under the hay barn roof.

Your dad's spade you said
was half-hafted
because he was short:

The tool you showed me was stubble-high too
but retained its keenness
because you oiled and ragged it.

I watch now as you cut
below your house
tipping concrete into the gap.

The fox bench you pass shows
loose shingles of sand
lacing the ground underneath.

ON LAKE WINDERMERE

From the back of our boat a wake line develops
which we watch angling backwards in a v;
two boys' eyes moved by movement.

Light plays its part too, with dizzying events
in the water ringing our bent scramble
along the surface.

The lake acts simply on the hull's lacquered joints
bouncing down hard into the cold
hangar of water.

CAR IN A FIELD

Corn stumps do homage to the wreck that blackens them.
Nipped off sections, a plate, some rubber and a ball of wire
litter ruts from the gate.

It was left to burn and stand while around it lay
a heated star-map of track marks, running to the spot
that found it ruined.

Other cars return from work to see its frame revved
under a crow calling. Strings of corn pull it down,
hunted, to the field's heart.

SPIDERS

From my fingers
five micro-spiders rise
on ascending parachutes.

In the light their strands
look like steam boiled from
my tips during a hot spell.

I am bound by their silk
to a flow of air
that asserts itself gently.

How they shift me to a place
where the lighter elements
churn and race.

Soon they unsnag themselves
allowing their threads
to catch the breeze

and then take off;
howling no doubt
but silent to me.

ORDINARY TIME

Through stained glass
there is more stained glass,
not quite at full dazzle, but illuminated.

A back-beaming sun
sneaks through its surface into the space behind,
then into the space behind that.

The biblical folk are obscured,
obviously lost somewhere in that harlequined gap.
Still, their glow remains,

no doubt
cheering the Evensong choir
as their precisely-sung soft canticles echo.

Here is the something of which we all dream:
A strong arm, gathered about a shoulder;
a voice heard over gravestones,

which double as scripted, firm-footed paving slabs.
Weighty are the blessings of those inside,
whose voices are amplified more than they think they are.

THE IMPROVEMENTS AT QUEENS PARK

Six-foot wire fences
protect us from the
lake's risen silt.

In places, undergrowth
is everywhere
spilling out onto the surface.

The goodwill of
the new flowers has gone,
replaced by strutting privet.

Death and peace are sucked
into a line of up-turned,
ploughed-up strips.

Foul, dog-leg of land,
somehow lost on the field,
never to be called back.

COME THEN ANGELS, LEAD ME FROM THE FALLING CITY

My heart
is plague-softened; rotten.
Nothing now is going to prevent
its collapse under the bulk
of this bleak winter call.

Worse, I am calling back; cold-calling,
frozen solid with the effort
of so much chat.

It's amazing
what noise can be drowned out by this chilly talk:
cars and birds; the folding of newspapers;
the casual psalms
to the usual.

So if here I come to it at last
at least I have come to it.
The ground will hold my bones as its own

and then blow them,
eventually,
to the four corners of the kingdom.
An eventful
eventual quartering.

And so I come to it,
enduring hourly calls, cold on the wind,
telling my body to come.

Yes.
A Saturday afternoon dangle,
lectern-angled from a tree,
will take torment
from this land;

which itself groans
with the weight of the same robe-white call.
But it can regenerate. I cannot.

It can sprout.
I cannot.
Or if I can, it is only to sprout
a toad eye; a worm skin;
a newt tail; a bat wing.

Frozen, ground-dwelling, called-to calling-creature:
Shamble through the trees.
Survive another night.

IF ONLY THE RAPTURE HAD COME THIS MORNING

I say these guardian words
in order to release the day:
'Morning scoot; Moon in its arc;
trees on their ground; magpie on an aerial.'

So the tooting, razzing day comes
with the speeding steroid pump of cars.

From black back bumpers, wights make their way skyward,
unfurling in the sodium of a street lamp.
They are silent, but move as if they are making
perpetual o's.

And oh! how they sway under bird wings,
getting tangled in phone wires lifting lithe on the breeze.

Tangled aerials, tangled wights.
Tangled crustal asteroid whiff of the road.
Tangled wights at the rear of a car;
tangled wights feeding at the tangled back of a car.

After this catastrophic tangling of form,
thick, slickly-gilled current raises everything Babylon-ward.

It's the end of the start of the morning,
everyone is heading for work.
The hump of the day is yet to come,
so let's hope for oblivion before then.

AGEING HARPOONER

I
Vanished blubber culture
of a dead whale
lapping at a shoreline;
photographed,
then mounted in bits
above a couch.

Its blunt bulk stretches
back out to sea
from a patron saint
to a saintless depth
of paintless blue,
cracked on the seabed.

II
Remnant bottle
of sperm whale oil
perches abandoned in a factory.

Its uses – lamp fuel, cosmetics
and nitroglycerine –
have moved on.

The slim glass is bound
by string and drizzled adhesive
which has eaten into the label:

GREMIO DOS ARMADORES DA
PESCA DA...
LISBOA – PORTUGAL
...edegacao de S. A Rog...

III

Senhora da guia, the patron saint of whalers,
is honoured with a procession.
She is held by three cherubs
riding on a cloud of cupped lilies.

She considers her journey
from church to harbour to carnival skiff
to water and then to another church,
plumed on a hill above another village.

Her sweet swaying face reminds the men
of the weeks of dying amongst unvarnished boat prows;
many of which now ply the harbour-dazzle
of a dozen lit up restaurants.

BUGGER PLATO

With your holding-down-kit you smite ladies
and have them giggling whilst gagging on
your feet. Teetering, your belly torpedoes
hopes of sex, yet you say you fancy a
bit and would take it from many of the
girls who stalk the estate, though a hard-on
would be hard on your heart, given your low
blood pressure and, diabetically-
speaking, you say taking on a local
lady would be too much trouble: One of
them might kill you while riding up on top.

At the end though, when it's suggested that
the old are renowned for sitting out this
non-sex-stage, you say nothing and you laugh
and your torpedo-end belly wiggles.

HAMMERED TREE

A shit-faced city tree sits smacked;
its branches dangle and bulge
and wordlessly rage.

Its itchy terrific sap spins.
Dirt rims its crotchless roots.
Its growth hangs in piss-yellow pockets.

This supreme target happens here;
stood against the winds' love,
stirred by what it can't have.

NANTWICH ON A THURSDAY

Market day calls the old to attend stalls
in search of damply stacked cups in boxes.

Grouped by the exit they chat
appalled by flies, angered by rags;
assured that crops hate their guts.

The bell-spanked indoor air sings
of them and those like them who
work to keep the dark hours dark.

In the trees around the square
children boil, making goofy decisions
with their soft feet.

They casually pepper the dead
lying fused with their metallic offerings.

THERE'S NO PITY IN THE MIST

Ghost litter of a man
trapped directly
in the act.

A definition
just as clear as
Man the Maker
is needed.

So.

Hanging Man.
Decapitated Man.
Slit Wrists Man.
Shot Himself Man.

The world at 13:13
is so simple;
the words
come like a brook
oilily throwing itself
down a shallow valley.

Empty thicket man;
heart-stinking,
brain-sinking,
hospital man,
moving in calamity,
feeding on calamity,
kneeling on calamity.

Calamity Man.

Calamity
which the children
will feel
though not know
until the tempest
of their emptiest of days.

YEAR OF THE COMET

I. DERELICT

Archaeopteryx-sprawling stone,
blistered and spread,
battered and worn,
shattered under a roof of red.

Think of the workmen that left here;
think of the machines piled up.
All of them touched by nothing less
than the circuit of a celestial object.

Ancient boulder-building;
comet-splinter;
dust-broken, star-struck wall.
Everything lies cratered and cracked.

II. ON THE LOST VISIONS OF POST-MEN AND POST-WOMEN

One evening, one summer,
a bobbled Visually Impaired flag-stone
lay flecked by fag ends.

The then-smokers were sat on plastic crates
and watched the long comet tail unpick the stars;
its revolting twinkle voiding into their eyes.

Cigarettes were lowered as the view was taken in.
Smoke was exhaled
in bilious thoughtful clouds.

Free hands that held brews in the cool air
would have happily held the arse of some other worker
whose deep blue pockets curved nicely when they bent over a machine.

Maybe something could be done about that later.
Meanwhile the electric tick of the comet's signal was transmitted,
even if no-one could hear it yet.

III. THE WORLD TURNED UPSIDE DOWN

On this latest lap, a mass of material was vapourised into space.
Its hardcore tabletop crust hissed dust into a tail 600,000 miles long
which formed a daft snake of light
registering not much more than a candle
turned upside down in a topsy-turvy church.

All was to be overturned.
I sat alone on a castle wall reading The Outsider.
I didn't go to work and I didn't eat.
As I sat, it became apparent
that all my old wing-whirrings were worn out.

Many other visitors had the bearing of beings
who continued to feel their beings being lifted by events.
Light and hot and at the tip of things,
they balanced on the same wall as countless insects
whose heads had been eaten out by other insects.

IV. OMENS

Overhead the rarest of hairy sun gods flamed on,
going out during the day, but reappearing in the dark.

That bright, hopping star was a void
for everything else to pivot around.

In the world before and the world after
probably almost everything was unchanged.

But something was changed; there were extinctions.
People were terrified, or they were delighted.

Either way, my blank vision-ravings lay everywhere altered
as the beard of ash-light returned to exile.

V. WHISTON'S VISION

Comets smash into the proto-solar system,
barrelling into targets
before there are barrels;
or targets.

Everything cools off; pebbles form,
pebbles become boulders, boulders become planets.
Then other planets come along
to smash everything up again.

A whole history of forming and reforming
(which incidentally can linked to the Old Testament).
A whole science which sides with the angels
(provided the angels are happy with gravity)

VI. IS THIS WHAT I SEE?

So this year I think of being old
before my time.
I think of my vapour trail
shaking like an atavistic tail;
a farted out, seventeenth century, throwback tail,
a quarter-of-a-yard long.

I am a brute-man, baboon-fooling,
cat-calling, dog-barking, bird-larking.
I claim dominion
over this comet-creation
by the act of enjoying a piano recital
then talking about it afterwards over finger biscuits.

Well, perhaps, but chimps are known to swing
around waterfalls,
sensing a spiritual something.
And ibises can navigate for miles over Africa,
taking alternate routes when needed,
making sure their roles rotate.

So if change comes via the means
of a movement of rock in space,
that change has been made
by an object. An object.
But then I suppose it will be an object that has smashed
and smashed and smashed this world into shape.

And, perhaps, occasionally the converse may be true:
that I may make a comet tremble too.
That I may trouble a comet with my injunctions.
My injunctions.
As potent as the injunctions
of an extinct bird.

BOMBERS OVER CREWE

Riding down West Street,
the bike rider sees immense gull-shadows
droning low over a workshop roof,
scattering their load along a train line.

She outruns the primary explosion,
getting over a bridge
before it lifts dust from benches,
making an airborne disc of pink and tan.

From her auntie's house she sees the crowds
flapping behind the bomb fumes;
she sees the injured carried out like ballast to fields
where bike frames halo a balloons' bolted cable.

The uninjured spread out, creating their own wraiths with fag smoke.
The space they jam is suddenly thick
with names that will forever be tethered
to the blast.

No-one wants to leave once the all-clear wails,
but an ancient-item-moving cold finally moves in;
it has sensed newly inanimate objects
lying amongst the girders.

TWO BROTHERS AND THEIR CANAL TREAT

We pitch up already pissed
onto the tow-path
thankful
that mooring ropes
appear to have shrunk.

Each barge drips
with colour and
hard-to-credit plants and
stacks of wine and
drunk indulgent faces.

Or is that us, reflected?!
Our path weaves through
this damp strip of countryside
that slopes not always
due to topography.

I get excited by a gap in a hedge
that opens up a conversation
about Civil War musketeers
battering each other
in a pre-canal field.

It's hard not to think
of the dirty ribbon
curling next to us
as having always
been there

feeding on rain;
exploding with dragonflies;
giving a family gang
of locals a chance
to fish and laze on grass.

After that deep insight
we curve under a bridge, fingering its grooves
before we relieve ourselves just past it
behind a mystery structure
glittering with carved, gold-lettered sex-graffiti.

Further up there's another structure,
this time of sinister water-boarded concrete
that'll need negotiation and of course
we wonder what secret course
its pipes and tubes take.

Our beer-craving speeds up our walking
yet we seem to go backwards:
time is definitely running slowly
as we pass one rusty pylon
more than once.

We're not arguing
but I am apologetic
as the heat is fierce,
the bugs are biting
and we really need booze.

We step it up.
At one point you actually start running,
which sets me off
huffing behind you,
stumbling over clumps of reed.

I was sure the pub was closer,
even though you assured me it wasn't.
We stagger further...
then there it is
our lit up sow,

suckling its piglet barges,
servicing its piglet people.
And we, grateful new piglets,
gobble up chips and onion rings
and beer and red wine.

LOVE IS TO BE FORGOTTEN

Sports divers gargle to the surface
iterating a love lost to this river.

Soldiers and villagers have cast in handfuls
remarkably unknown to one another:

A six-inch fishing harpoon of cut bone;
a set of clasps; a socketed axe; a plastic bin lid.

All are brought up and brought to account
through a broth of liquid and re-breathed air.

Any objects rasped from this silt
sit odd in the hand before being boxed.

But they are triumphs of disturbance;
breaking the calm of this picture-water

that grasps its antiques that were antiques
even before they were pitched in.

JOURNAL OF A PLAGUE YEAR: WELLS GREEN

Bone flakes fill the vet's wall
just where the traffic lights are;
just where a blind poet on a horse
might have paused, sensing his guts drop
as he moved onto this blustery
cloud-clinkered strip of road.

Wells Green. The horse stumbles
breaking wind on a broken pavement.
The car chokes at the lights.
Look around at the brick hides
of the crossing; look at the poplars,
bi-polar in their swaying and standing still.

Wells Green greens well.
What a vessel to tip a life into:
The road and the lights;
the cars farting their engines,
loaded with banned footballers
and future adulterers.

Life tosses itself off.
The horse stamps under the poet
who squints all four ways before crossing.
Death has been this way,
squirting its dirt at the undertakers on the opposite corner,
but not nearly as much as it should have been doing.

Nowhere near enough slaughter. Nowhere near enough
of the nailing of doors shut has happened here.
This crossroad has swaddled its crossers,
who have come from the vets with their animals
sidestepping the more traditional
chains of being.

Vested, long-beaked, lamb-footed crossers,
expert at turning food into shit and
expecting the expected.
They profess their cures to be cures
even as they fall with their preservatives
still in their mouths.

AWAKE

Spider-hearted boy,
whose night-time crawling hands
grow inflected by sleeplessness.

You sleep for the dangling queen of the evening
sure as she is about what should be.

But now your banging head will not let you settle;
foaming, fuming, volcanic soul;

dream-singed, desperately convulsing;
as shocked as Earth on pole-shift day.

In the morning, your hand-print in frost on the car
leaves five ovals and a rounded wedge.

Six eye-holes for light to get through to the cold interior
which persists damp to the touch and deeply black.
Tonight you must sleep, sleep, sleep, sleep.

STARVING TIME

Portions of a maid
lie in a seventeenth century cellar,
trashed with an unwanted deposit
of imported worms.

Four closely spaced marks
in her forehead indicate
a failed attempt to split open the skull
to get at the brain.

Finally, it seems, the back of her head
was cracked open with a light-weight axe or cleaver.
Fragments from the scene were splintered everywhere;
most had numerous saw-tooth marks.

Almost definitely this was not done
by an experienced butcher.
There are however signs of one or more assailants
interested in the muscles of the face:

Cheek meat, tongue and throat tissue
were gouged with the tip of a knife
being worked along the lower jaw.
The inedible hair they left in place.

Mercifully, all these cut and chop marks
suggest she was already dead
or they'd be more haphazard;
presumably because she'd have been fighting back.

Isotopes show that her teeth were washed
by the groundwater of southern England.
The levels of nitrogen that her diet was high status –
either as a daughter or as a servant who pinched meat off the plates.

80% of the population died here.
Everyone suffered and nothing was spared.
Not even the dead, who were dug up
to be licked dry by dry dying tongues.

THE WHALE

Look again at this shadow
formed behind tins
on the kitchen wall.

Nothing contains it
yet it has boundaries
which it cannot flout.

It is oblong,
fading towards the top
as the light strengthens,

lensed by kettle steam,
which blooms
as a tight line

thickening at the top
where a silver strip angles
presumably reflected off a shelf.

Rotund black
confinement
of form.

In itself it is deep form
and admits the end
that waits for us all.

Lying in love
recovering from some
devastation or weakness

we must find hope
where often
there is only vacancy.

TWO SHAKESPEAROES TALKING ON THE STAIRS

We stand in a stairwell
discussing Henry IV –
you've seen it live; I've
seen a Globe production
on the telly whilst ironing.

I liked the rude bits;
especially when a blow job
was suggested
by a roll of white doublet
flopped into a pint pot.

Shakespeare isn't something
I've truly laughed at to be honest.
Apart from a joke I heard years ago,
I think by Mercutio,
about pricks at midday.

Our chat wasn't all about
seventeenth century drama-porn though.
We did discuss witchcraft and
the changing role of Banquo,
possibly altered for James I/VI.

You then mentioned
how the speeches were deliberately worded
so the groundlings could hear
the goings on
on the raised stage.

At that point I remarked that I'd seen a source
from the sixteenth century,
from a Spanish ambassador,
which mentioned in passing
players being at court for Queen Elizabeth.

It referred to her black teeth,
and her tired-looking pearls.
But then I added that as this was a Spanish view
it was bound to be
less than complimentary.

So it wasn't all rude oral talk
shuttered by a
blue-framed fire-door,
whispered before someone
respectable came past.

When someone respectable did come past,
we carried on.
All they could muster
was that the latest literacy strategy
was 'rolling out well'.

You managed 'bathos'
once the surprisingly shapely legs had climbed past.
I managed 'bollocks'.
Then the music teacher turned up
wanting volunteers for his choral group.

BIG GOD OF WAR

Wonder at the wondrous art of these brother-killers,
who force-feed lightning into each-other's veins
and lava into each other's lungs.

When the shell struck and the walls collapsed
you must have thought about leaving them
with an excuse already forming in your mouth.

The wonder is that you went back
to dig them out, expertly, with miner's hands,
pulling them from bricks burning in the man-fat-stinking smoke.

Later, mud must have clung to your gaiters
in yards of blown trench when you dug a second time
to rescue more boys who the ground did not want to give up.

By then your vision would have been blood-blunted,
your ears cloth-stuffed by the screams.
Yet you will have dug again and again,

in the sure knowledge that all of them
would soon be compost under the grass
however much you shovelled.

After all that you became a lay preacher and I wonder
how many then you were trying to dig from the landslip of sin;
a fang-corked wolf, dressed in white.

LITTLE GOD OF WAR

The dog chant behind your eyes
becomes mythic anger
as everything unravels in your head.

Nothing more serious than trousers
has unleashed this incinerator boy
on the stairs.

Everything is kicked, blunted, chucked, grabbed and throttled
in a wretched civil war
of one temper against another.

Oh I played my part, fanning the flames;
unleashing my own battle cry from the kitchen table
to the threshold you bash.

So what am I?
Fighting lightning-rod for your fury?
A moody black muse thirst quencher?

Boy born face down,
I am the soothing song sung into the darkness
within earshot of your fierce ancestors.

THE PESTILENCE

1. BURIAL OF PLAGUE VICTIMS AT TOURNAI

Immediately dug graves,
probably at the cusp of a settlement
or perhaps at the limits of a graveyard
hit hard by the dying;
the land is dimpled by burial.

Mouths which lovingly uttered words
unutterably loll,
sometimes under wood,
sometimes under a shroud
stained yellow and red.

Feet, bound by this maggot-cloth,
are walled by a high-backed earth.
Often they lie on other bundles
already pupating under lime;
moving the way dead things move.

2. BECAUSE OF THE MORTALITY

Plague victims at Tournai
are buried immediately,
sometimes by four burly mourners;
sometimes by one, heaving the corpse-weight
on a thick-set shoulder.

Some of these dead were wrapped in a shroud
that betrayed their slender form:
Thin in the middle,
head bulging at the top,
feet curled up at the bottom.

For them there was no wood left,
so they were cocooned in square grub-holes
almost in the same simple state as they came into the world.
They will leave when the wielded beak-stick
finally draws them back into the light.

NO SYMPATHY FOR THE DEVIL

Jagger starts
but its me getting excited,
pawing at my steering wheel,
not the fourteen-year-olds garbling in the back.

The sods.
But how can they rebel against rebellion?
Start little red books and institute a fire-breathing
New Culture to destroy the Old Culture?

Hm, doubtful.
All this connectedness,
all this photographing and filming,
will put a stop to the violence that entails.

Book burnings can't be made public nowadays.
And if there's torture, victims will always have the last say
if their torment is accompanied by a saved picture
dotted with sadface.

Their best bet is to gabble about jumpers,
not being hungry since Christmas Eve
and whether a friend was a slag or not
doing a boy in a bush at a party.

They're also best ignoring the old goat
singing in a daft American accent.
Or indeed, the old goat currently pursing his lips
in sync with the old goat singing in a daft American accent.

After I'd given the lift, my soundtrack for ironing was:
Anything Nirvana, followed by No Pussy Blues,
followed by The Gravediggers Song,
Doolittle and then The Cramps.

Rock and Roll Mayhem.

SPENDING TIME UP ST. WERBURGH'S STREET

Life is short
Filled with stuff
Don't know what for
I ain't had enough.

I. SHOPPING

Down the river float crosses tied to logs;
old blessings for an old goddess.

For a new goddess people float past windows
being blessed by sequinned dummies.

There is nothing more complex here than feet
adjusting to bulges in the street.

Permissive, pram-swaggering shit-stains,
busily budding their new worlds.

Where a shadow bangs its heel hard across the road,
these happy shoppers cross and merge with the light of the other side.

II. ANGLING THE SLICES

Off bulbs hiss on a dangle of wires swinging above a great fake Tudor front.
All day, swan-necked road arrows have shifted cars right.
Dimensions here are small slack dimensions caught
between the kerb and the stuffed waste-grip of the dripping grids.
It'd be nice to walk down here pissed, but time shuffles the axis of the street
and folds
the moment neatly away along with a set of flowers shedding in the
cathedral beds.

III. REQUIEM FOR THE HERMIT OF ST WERBURGH'S ABBEY.

Phantoms build around heeled-in earth,
keen to remember a dismembered king.

His hermitage shed wood flexes against stone.
His arrow timber rests washed on a ledge.

Long lost king, remember yourself now
as your remains are tilled into the ground;

as your first thoughts
become your last thoughts;

as lesser men survive and travel east
to cut their names into high church stone.

LYRICS
CRAMPS - NEW KIND OF KICK

YET ANOTHER ONE ABOUT DEATH

Rhetoric of the world exhausted,
the grass overhead grows
muddy as always,
as water seeps down
to your turned around bones.

You create your own angles now,
without pit-props
or the need to blast anything.
The weight has come on
but you don't need pulling from it.

Your Zeus-wrath is with me still,
and your predator-love of the Zulus.
How I could do with your calmer side though.
Stir, my lord of the ground, stir;
rest your moth-backed hands on my shoulders.

WALK ACROSS A CAR PARK IN NOVEMBER

This year's omens continue,
smuggling themselves in under the flickering
now-you-hear-it, now-you-don't
sob of a motorbike struggling over speed bumps
set out on the other side of some new-builds.

Via text I learn that overnight a friend dreamt of crosses
before waking up to owl hoots at two in the morning.
Apparently when she slid out of bed she thought she saw
people talking in the corner of her room.
She dismissed them with a piss.

It's cold as I walk from the car;
each step involves water soaking through my right sole
which has turned into Hoover-leather
since I forced the shoe on with the laces tied last week.
Almost without knowing I act like I did when I was nine.

Even my soap-soaked sponge crotch-rub in the shower
that morning was reminiscent of me then, hoiking myself up
penis-first, onto the banister and gyrating
with the thought of a girl playing netball in my head.
The same urges, the same sensations, the same actions.

Well, without the banister. Or the girl. Or netball.
It then crossed my mind how the world hurricanes us
to harbours we didn't expect to be in,
to people we didn't expect to be with. But there our world is,
revealed in the same way as the sun as it comes out from behind a cloud.

I crunch a stone into some mud
slopped around the impact cracks
of a shallow pothole.
This morning, like most mornings these days,
is going to be a monumental ball-ache.

GENTLEMAN'S OFFICE

In the noumenal world of the toilet cubicle
sound is lord:

Door swing; strip light bang;
urine splash; hand wash splash;
door hinge groan; belt slither; shit splash,
shit splash, shit splash, shit splash;
shuffle; flush; door; light ping.

Nothing but noise experience comes into my cave
until I stand up to sort myself out.

On the black plastic toilet tank
a fine white paint has been sprayed,
and it's a spit of the cosmos.
I consider that, then stick my hand into the bog water
to clean away my skid marks.

Then I'm off to be briefed
about a different kind of shit.

WHITE LIGHT

Lit-up roof-lights dot a rooftop
at a quarter-to-eight, when already
the day feels washed out.
A bushel of old Christmas lights
foams on a low-slung front eave.

Oh Birther! Father-Mother of the cosmos

There are also stairwell lights:
industrial, disked, streaking
through oblong glass;
potent in their locally-sourced
building-gloom.

Focus your light within us – make it useful

The grey of the roof felt
picks out all their flashings.
The grey of the sky
then oppresses them,
sheeting terribly.

Out of you, the astonishing fire

Later the view improves
as the atmospherics intensify.
This new light untangles
the upper knots
of a rectangular sports hall.

Your heavenly domain approaches

I move to the other side of the building
spreading my hands on a fiery sill.
My breath mists up a portion of window.
Sol Invictus becomes a bald circle
emptied onto glass.

VILLAGE ON THE FROST ROAD

I

Still, silent, air-lugged land. Quite empty, save
for a stock of perfectly swaying fields.

I drive at an even pace, taking in scenes
I've taken in countless times before:

A massive canister of a tree trunk,
rolled across the gate of a gypsy stop site;

two bridges over a brown blown-glass canal
wheezing through a strip of steaming yards;

several white-topped pre-fab houses on a bend
that bear the brunt of the road and hiss out heat.

At a corner I see a tractor with no driver.
Perhaps they've been whisked away by the Rapture;

or perhaps they've been whisked away by whirring claws
to live in terror in the shell of the soil.

It doesn't much matter which; either way
I am stuck in the land of the dead.

II

Some of the dead it seems think they are not stuck.
Some are travelling in an air of panic back along the road
in vehicles or on foot with dogs
panting on leads.

There's a man on a bike.
There's someone in a black car
who whistles and stops to pick up a walker
with a carapace of newspaper jammed under his coat.

These would-be exiles
fancy themselves reprieved and exhaled by whatever sucked them here.
Perhaps they have been reprieved.
But they haven't been exhaled.

They huff and seek an inspired escape,
but it's clear that they have been given short shrift.
The ground is colder than they thought and their destination more remote.
Their cars have ceased to billow, just as they have ceased to billow.

III
At the heart of it all
a breathless slumberer
has made the world still.

For her, life has been measured in fistfuls of earth;
or measured as time drifting without the adjunct of love;
or measured as floats around the churchyard yews.

Engine gargle vibrates the granite-lunged gargoyles
but it cannot shake up the goings-on in that small plot
allocated just behind the main gate.

No, no reversal.
The slumberer's heart
slumbers on under a pile of chilled paper flowers.

IV
So, the silver birches here are stuck being silver;
the zinc alloy lamps are stuck being zinc alloy.
Always and forever, even if they lean towards the vicarage,
where it's only right to expect a miracle or two.
Although the last one came in 1984
when there was an award for best kept village.

The sign was screwed behind a renovated black pump –
'Best Kept Village 1984.' And it seems time stopped then,
or perhaps just before then.
Since when there's been no wind, no breath, nothing burbling on the green.
No pine trees caressed blissfully by blue breezes.
No inflation; not even of tiny swags of grass
swished into wisps by insect legs.

Of course the church bell still rings.
But the bell master and his wife are both dead,
gone within a year of each other; their business taken by tuberculosis.
Gone too is the sanguine barber surgeon, ushered out by a surfeit of unshed
blood.
Gone, dead and fixed forever beneath a troublesome sprite-spirited Spring-
time sarsen.

The bell rings and a bustling boy side-winds to school, late, crisis-skinned;
several thought bubbles shushed under a stream of woollen hair.
He tokes on an inhaler then shoves it in his plump red bag,
ready to wag it in the faces of his teachers.

V
Cold condenses to white
on the peaked point of fences;
on opulent stones dug up and sat upright;
on useless smeared cars;
on an exhausted angel-site.

Now someone has belted up the bell.
The sorries on everybody's breath
have been said. Do not be still then slumberer, do not be still.
Valve your vapours from the surface of the earth,
let this village exhale.

DEE SONG

Floodwater tips downstream
to strike this point of boats,
slipping on hulls caught
in the thick river silt.

Alluvial, hardened, built on;
the shoreline is readied for
the steamy piss house with its
low blue light.

By the Anchorite terrace
you drop your bike on its
axles and watch a stag night
settle on a line of benches.

Rub shoulders now with old men;
let spit build in your mouth.
Go to the river to see your mobile
comet-face flopping on the surface.

AN ANIMAL WITHOUT A BRAIN CAN STILL SNEEZE

I

Iron bird feeder, like a Greek helmet's
twin-curved sheen,
or an absurd Surrealist machine.

Its two fat-and-seed-filled coconuts
have a testicular hang –
somewhat like yin and yang.

Behind them the modern world sings:
Chimney, aerial, phone wire,
yucca and satellite spire.

Behind that the somewhat more ancient
neighbour
of clouds, sky and vapour.

II

The flocked feather life that visits today
is corpulent and clumsy
to the point of comedy.

Great Tit, Blue Tit, Robin,
Long Tailed Tit, Blackbird and Pigeon.
Falling again and again.

I feel their insistent grumble
gurning at my window.
I see also how

the water drips
from each branch
to each reach

of metal or wood
that claws its way, less
due to consciousness

than to the fact
that it must
simply exist.

III

Clouds, sky and vapour,
so insistently
banging their big blue belly.

It's Sunday and the rumble of a bin
colludes with the rumble of music's
airborne mathematics.

Somewhere above
an astronaut is nearly drowned
on a spacewalk by a doom-domed

faulty helmet.
He will be glad to see the Earth
again, maybe next month.

Near him – near the foot of Perseus –
the California nebula, NGC 1499,
persists as barely a sign

in our vision because of its diffuse nature,
low density and red light
(which our eyes struggle with at night).

All these wrong wavelengths.
Ah well, it's likely
that it's only lit up by a light blue giant nearby.

Yin and Yang and gravity,
when allied to the world of daylight,
speak of birds and of bird flight.

THE ANDREWS DIPTYCH

Ivory, once clasped by a golden hinge,
lies now as two parts with a common edge.
Miracles are dished out in each section;
six wonders of faith, wondrously given.

This relicless relic has persisted
as the stone walls around it have crumbled.
Its holy tables became weed-wrangled
long after it was smuggled and shifted.

Men without faith would have held it, gasping
at the unbearded man's calm wand-waving.
Lepers; the blind; the hungry; those in need
of a drink to secure a wedding bed.

Those without faith continue to hold it,
gawping at the credulity of unlit
faces, prepared to see the living dead
stagger back through sand to their living land.

The awed faces of these sculpted tusk men
maintain a cloud-hushed, simple expression.
The world behind them retains its velvet
off-white of heaven; its solid bone of spirit.

HIS MASTER'S VOICE

(For ALW)

1. SWALLOWED

Morning again
where my scene
isn't one of sudden
heart failure.

Is it right
to be wishing for it
when a girl has been found
dumped in a canal and

a toddler drowned
in a pool after a
bang to the
head?

What is it exactly
that I'm wishing for?
Cessation?
Moving on?

There's a small fly
trapped in my throat
from a mouthful of wine
I didn't really check last night.

Its final moments
must've included some kind
of heavenly bug vision;
some kind of drift towards a light.

Hm… 'Its final moments':
Barely perceptible breath;
a slowed heart;
an intangible shift of weight;

a borrowing of energy
from the next world
to keep this one going
a little while longer.

A borrowed
pocket of energy;
taken,
but paid straight back.

2. A DOG SHITTING IN THE AFTERNOON

It's Saturday again, with wedding bells
bonged for a white tribe in Rollers.

They make me consider time ebbing
as I sort this, my latest excrescence,

to the sounds of mock gunfire
banging clean on kitchen walls.

3. FINAL ORDERING OF THOUGHTS ON HER IN THE OLD GARDEN

Bird skeleton,
bright under feathers,
yearns in the evening on
a fence as the evening disappears.

Its call is odd,
nowhere near the bluster of Spring,
when four-square churchyard
air takes the sound for miles.

It is a dark light-weight patch
on an otherwise clear sky
that digests worms in a catch
from the soil.

There's a loose sense of order
this late in the day.
There are just suspicions, under
the heavier branches, of movement.

Where once she picked at self-seeded
weeds, caught between two sheds,
there is now only concrete, stained
red by wet trampoline spring rust.

4. VANISHED BY NIGHT

Ague in the bone
of having had enough:

bone-white
on blood red –

the constant bloom
on the table

an offering
of table manners

where manners are best left
somewhere else –

caved
in the desert.

5. KEYWORDS

Steady yourself. Listen
to the flapping of paper-gusts
turning pages in the wind.

Blinds bay above the glass, grinding at times in time
with a blown tin can rattling in the street.
This is invisible hand movement.

Here things that change twin with things that don't.
They combine thick and fast, jammed up
in the gush of the classroom.

A French peasant revolutionary; an Auschwitz inmate;
Feudalism; détente; civil war; The Dissolution;
cave paintings; Senlac Ridge; a plague doctor.

The long history of the intellect
drawn over a carpet
heaped with A4.

How many dead people
I have spoken to in these four walls.
How many dead people have I spoken to?

How many men and women,
who stopped me on corridors
or stared out from my window?

There's a noise outside in the bushes,
shushed man-like sounds; but there is no man.
A blackbird flies out calling.

The wind has stopped gusting now,
the flapping paper has died down.
It is silent around the school.

6. TRAPPED DIVER

A scientist gasps on a long lost cord
in a shake-down dive into a blue hole.

Only the pressure waves of current shift
the silt now; or perhaps the bulging touch
of released gas bubbling in the deep.
Nothing can move too quickly or nothing moves.

Too much leg-work will shatter the roof
or lead to a tangle in a tight crack.

Here a tortoise struggled and drowned;
there the crocodile that followed it down snapping.
The emptied remains jumble pristine on the floor
with owl wings and lizard jaws.

And in that calendared mess a full human forearm,
a torch, a flipper and a sheathed wetsuit knife.

Nearby the head, with scuba mask retained,
is a cauldron of eaten-out tissue.
Softly the hole mouth has digested it.
Slowly it has returned it to its pre-birth state.

It is a tribute collected from those who float
in the drowned, sunless, moonless dark.

7. HIS VOICE WAS LIKE A DOG WHISTLE

Crow rah over roofs,
calling over children searching
for their too-long-gone parents.

There's a chance they've run from the screams
that bounce everywhere these days.
But they're still here,

preventing the unhinging
of their lives with stolen,
boozed-up moments in the kitchen.

So scream children, if that'll do you any good.
Scream and bounce off the walls
at the top of the stairs.

Water is draining into the sewers,
the day is subsiding under crow scrapes and
jackdaw jumps in the gutters.

This vision even vision doesn't understand is in tatters.
But what is known is that although there's nothing left to void,
there is still the act of voiding itself.

THE FOREVER FEELER

Water for the living
water for the dead.

Tonight's dreams are going
to talk earth;

will see a slashed white form
through a window.

How I nestled next to you
speaking,

wrapped in the ground
with its woken flowers.

Tonight I will have the capacity
to accept dragons.

A form will move through the house –
browned fingers

gripping.
It will move without walking.

Spectral knot of knives, curdled
right where I must sleep.

Where I must sleep
awash with the spectre

of cosmetics shot through
with the cosmos.

I detect no order
in the laid out

multiple worlds
of fabric.

Or, if order,
only the goblin-order of speech.

NOT QUITE THE BATTLE OF NANTWICH

Last orders were spent with a blue-capped Covenanter
who had relegated himself to taking pictures of the weekend's action.
He just didn't fancy the rugby with sticks
of the less complicated men
who were signed up for the King and could piss
hands-free whilst discussing Civil War pike tactics at length.

Outside wet snow was falling, flooding the river
as we slopped over the bridge in inappropriate footwear.
Its banks were forced as in 1644,
but there was no slaughter in the frozen fields,
or hammering in the hedgerows,
or crack-pot shooting at Acton church.

But then again, in the recesses of square-glassed shop fronts
a fervour was growing
between a blonde girl in a micro-mini
and some unseen man who was partly mumbling in Welsh
and partly mouthing some Presbyterian battle-hymn.
Both of them used the word 'cock' and 'punch' a lot of times.

We had more pacific urges to attend to with the draw of cheesy chips
from the Swine Market takeaway, so we wandered off.
When we wandered back we found a small tough-looking woman,
who was expertly clad for cold, hailing taxis
in the manner of a Suffragette
pinning a rosette on a horse.

When a cab did turn up, there was some horse-trading
between her and a fair-minded girl
who had waited her turn, refusing to flash her granny tights.
They eventually filled a small saloon, whilst us three beery men
reversed muskets and battered ourselves onto a different sticky back seat,
where we talked seventeenth century politics and galloped back through the
night.

ON THE ELECTRIFICATION OF THE CULTURAL QUARTER

Sloppy clay clag
forms a vacuum so complete
our tugging tool blades struggle.

I'm chipping the corner of a slab
while the new father-in-law and step-son
lump-hammer nails and saw through pales
blistered under blue paint.

Clod-steeped water
peels the baked brick base of the house,
flood-grooming its hard underside
until it crumbles.

Future children will see the sods we leave in the loam
and conclude that there was human activity here.
There'll be no dint in the threshold
where a chicken has roosted.

Neither will there be a head -
plastered and poked into the ground
with shells in its eye-holes -
sat on coiled-up treasure.

A snake of armoured wire
will be our continuing presence,
laid out under slats
for the protection of new diggers.

Persistence here
comes as a column of mud
spiralling down to the centre of the Earth.

YOU, ME AND THE GARDEN

We spread a knuckle of seed
mending the garden's mineral-devoid ground.

Bits of oak flock,
once captives of the air,
lie leaf on leaf
as we pinpoint spots to lie clay on clay.

Forgiveness is a speciality of this soil,
burying its monsters at the foot of a maze-rooted apple-blossom tree.

We too are good at burial.
But lately also at discovering those good plants
that somehow survive celebrating
in the boggy borders.

FINISHED CROW

This is a wrongly extended
bush-caught
crow.

A hedge-crow
solarised by a thin light leaking
through the ripped joints of its feathers,

which have been
pushed and pulled up
to a higher-than-normal angle.

High adaptation has here led to a trap
for flank, abdomen, mantle, back, rump,
breast, throat, bill, claws and crown.

Thicketed dry black tick
whose slowly beaten wing flaps
have softly flowed to this standstill.

This is the mightiest of matter,
stuck in a crackling brash
over a famished song-post.

Heretical branches
unbend, unsway,
under the dry weight.

DRAGONFLY HUNTING

My world is splinters
spread over a moment
fragmented
into a thousand moments.

A bee not caught, but swatted away;
a bluebottle clipped loudly in mid-air.

I follow an aerial route resonating
with past dragonfly action.

Patience, ducking and then a serene swerve
over the head of a balding creature
whose species is too young
to count as food.

FOUR SONGS OF THE SEA

1. THE ISLE OF THE DEAD

In a breath of wind I am delivered wrapped
upright to this rock. I sense the bobbing
hull in the swell and taste the augury smoke.

Figures indicate my coming and slide
into the water, raising me ceramic-head-first
to walk on its surface as I'm brought in.

I am hauled to my spot, cool and dark
under a poplar. A man-made precinct,
arranged to face the cemetery road.

2. VIEW OF THE FLOOD

He sees a land reached only by water;
its bitter pitched roof-tops rising from sand;
its green-skin sheds standing evenly drenched,
openly rocking and steaming in the air.

In its yards, blasted peg basket colours lie
scattered over slate or spread piecemeal
from the base of a rearing plaster horse
shearing mud from each speckled weed.

A form behind a door undeniably
gives a blurred early warning of movement.
Beyond everything life remains,
even as the final walls are taken by water.

3. LEGACY WORK

The smooth pink trio on the beach
are called into being by a picture.
From the lower rocks they watch the tide
as it rolls over cold marine sand.

Where the sea stalls is a land bridge
linking the hotel-deep mainland
to the rigged boulders they thought
had dragon eyes and drowned dragon jaws.

Paddling forms lost to the world
at the one moment they existed,
shaping the beach clay with their feet
as arriving waves ceased to be waves.

4. SUNKEN SHIP

Rippling structure, curled tightly
under a flow pattern of fish,
calls out its side-snapped rods
and holed tank boxes.

Finally sent to the coral,
cannon muzzles choke on pink sponge;
hatches grow assured of their special
shape by a gradual build-up of reef.

An average inundation drops
from a water column
to this thread-depth
with its held, blue minutes.

Spilt mechanisms shift and accrete,
fathoming the drippy wheel
that brought them down
to these cemented tomb-yards.

HE SAYS HEAT DEATH

Lips like death
appear opposite,
smeared purple.

Those two plum strips
fly apart equally, but fly back
smacking together –

dark belt-black and
comically luminous with wine
drunk from a tea cup.

Galaxies in my time have been torn up,
their heat and light burned out,
the darkest of matter accelerating everything.

Worlds above have fallen repeatedly
in as many quasi-, pseudo- and cool-rips
as you can shake a shitty stick at.

And yet the cats' self-absorbed chair-suck goes on,
spine-arch gracefully attuned
to whatever point of light has turned up overhead.

Aldebaran, Hyades, Pleiades.
Alnitak, Alnilam, Mintaka.
In fact, any other concoction you like:

The Follower;
The Central One;
The White Girl.

When I arch my back to look up again later
I'm even more hammered
so I like the sound of 'Penis Piss',

'Squat Thrust',
'Long Tailed Tit Binary' or
'Giants Massive Cock Cluster'.

They're all OK;
their shared fate
being to someday explode.

SKELETON CHAMPION

The eyes are stripped
under a red prism;
an aether of red light coming into existence
blood shot, blood shod.

Here is the body flayed,
veins brought to the outermost layer;
the definitely-not-a-pig's-liver
is a down-turned meat-flower.

Find it senseless.
Find portions of it conveyed and
potted in any of four corners.
Four pointless portions.

Examine then
your venesection
of unwrapped veins;
gift your knife to it,
haul up its loops
to present a better bled cadaver.

This is a cupped corpse,
bulkily prone in its crimson skin.
Here is the open offer;
the access to all bodily satins,
all stains, all fine filaments and fibres.

Let this barked body gristle droop
the way a flower droops,
still attached to its stem
after a botched deadheading.

ASPIC

How we pick at this land,
hitting the chilled water table hard as we cut
square exact pieces of turf
re-laying them with a slight curvature;
a green spine wagging
from wall to gate threshold.

As our ground is spade-sliced
words fly from the soil
shrieking an old way of life
that circled sumps and bike oil
and actually needed candles
and street parties in dry fields.

Geese collide overhead
as they have for years.
The weather they flap through gets heavier
soon wrapping white around the streets
allowing scope for the lead scrape
of boots to pepper it.

Long suffering sticks of bone,
buried, stuck and tethered,
search upwards for cool lanes of air
milled by the surface blades.
New scars break the old;
a new top sits on old tops.

WHALEFALL

A descent so sweet
I feel I could stop it with a touch;
make it hover mid-plume.

I'd say it was falling
into a nightmare,
but I'm not so sure.

The twisting poetry of hagfish
is fuelled in the dark
by bundled fat.

Darkness at this depth must be constant.
Pressure must smash every sense senseless
so that there can be no looking round.

There is nothing to consider
but the brutal mouth and the noise
of the brutal mouth.

SURPRISE FACTOR IN HOW STARS DIE

Her exquisite silver sparkling lower lip
weaves a special spherical music into the air.

She is bewildered,
spending the last few days
padding barefoot over hot slabs.

Stood in the empty frame of her back door,
close observation shows she has empty cupboards.

Her mass-loss is also evident
with outer layers of dust-rich gas
being puffed slowly off.

Any movement sends the heavier elements
spinning away from her sacked breasts.

Polluting and enriching the atmosphere,
she is leaving a little something
for future generations to work with.

She reaches down for a wooden peg
fallen from her washing.

A metallic green eiderdown
buffets her shoulders
crashing itself on her head.

She pushes it away, emerging into a new world.
A strimmer has started up,

it's strangled call filling her yard.
And there's a couple
hammering clout nails into shed roofing felt.

The male is fat and huffs as she unlids the bin
to dump specks of spent matter. She is becoming dazed,

her mouth making a sound to match
the bouncing tool howl
knocking against her back wall.

She pursues the spiralling clothesline once more;
soon she will become its satellite.

HOW TO BURY THE UNDEAD

Other burials can be in winding sheets
dropped simply into the earth,
but any vampire corpses should be dropped
fang-first into a heavy wooden coffin.

The suspect remains
should be staked,
with several eight-inch-long iron spikes
driven through neck, pelvis and ankle.

Heads must also be severed
then rested on their legs,
as no decapitated individual
can rise from the grave.

In one recorded exorcism,
an elderly woman was found
with a moderate-sized brick
wedged into her mouth.

In another, a man had his head and upper leg bones
laid out in a skull-and-crossbones pattern.
So look out for handy ballast material
whilst making a study of pirate flags.

Some say that likely candidates
may well be unlucky sufferers
of tuberculosis or consumption,
whose pale, thin and wasted away forms

just happen to be like those of
a creature of the night
desperate to feed
on their neighbours.

They might add that in the grave
during the process of decomposition,
rigour mortis eventually disappears
resulting in flexible limbs,

just like a vampire.
Their gastrointestinal tract
will also have decayed producing a
dark, innocent fluid easily mistaken for fresh blood.

So they might not actually be one of the undead.
But then again...they might be a postprandial Drac.,
dozing in the soil with high blood sugars,
waiting for night to reappear.

COLLAPSED TREE

Rain directs the pencil smell of a snapped
yew into caravans and car vents.

A canopy has flopped, its burst
orange wood cheering at the sky;

past, violent action in places
opening a sub-world of fibre.

Its edgy, partner-fence lies exposed too
with straight ginger bits spread by the fall.

Crows and gulls scrape the forked remains,
searching and scrapping over fragments.

COSMIC COINCIDENCE AND INTUITIVE NON-NATURALISM
(Or On Why I Must Make Sense)

I

The sound here
Of the World at work.

Infinity spat through a chimney pot:
Cars; birds fighting over a spot;

Cars; workers digging something up;
Something that sounds like geese,

Or a donkey, or a dog
Dragged from the back of a car.

Then the smell.
Oooh, how that gets in,

Right in, and takes us back
But also forward;

It's stasis, right. Affinity in fact
For a place, for a project.

II

This is the mountain
To come down from

With fragments.
Now is the time.

What comes next
Is deeper than tombs.

Deeper than a seabed
Infested with sculpture.

III

Hear me, oh pigeons.
Oh ancestral pigeons.

Someone will get this
Knowing what comes next.

Infinity resides in a squiggle of ink.
Number without number,

Faces of the circular cosmos;
A hearth and a removal of eyes.

Eyes removed and resown
Deeper than tombs.

Or maybe resown in a stew,
Along with toads, eels and worms.

Anything liminal really;
Even that blackbird shitting.

Here is the birdcall of an age,
Hanging on a car horn

That hangs over a fence
Snaggled by honeysuckle.

IV

I constantly size up the space
I am about to leave

Making peace with people
(I've always been making peace with people).

How do I end?
How do I end

When there is no ending?
No structure to ending?

No spiral. No constant.
No need like the shitting need.

V

Angel shape in the hedge,
Bike wheel vision on the gravel,

Spiral off, but there is no spiral.
Only light: squeezed, pushed, pricked and teleported.

Light that was here at the start,
Was lost for a decade, then came back

Caught on a wing.
Let me impose marvels on these things.

My blue mind is reified
By the rain flopping on the flowers.

SCHOOL SKULL

Real
human skull,
pulled free
from a pile
of other skulls.

Sheep eye-sockets
appraise it.
Goat horns
knock flakes
from its holed
upper jaw.

Here
is the need
to be seen
even when the head
is a robbed-out ditch.

Luckily,
after laughing
with two science teachers,
today it will be seen
by children
being taught trepanning.

It will have
a crown of paper
on my desk
and they will see it
but not touch it.

In the evening,
in the cupboard,
the skull will settle
in its carrier bag
waiting; eyeless
in the dark.

CALDEY ROADS

It's out here we recover.
Three bitten heads bathed by saline spraying
from a high, brine-washed bow.

Our boat soothes the swell of this polite sea field,
swinging into dock
with its hungry motors gunning.

Where prehistoric travellers climbed with trouble
we slide on jetty seaweed,
remembering our way to the lighthouse.

Last time we were here the path
shimmered with life.
Now dry grass lines either bank.

Further up, under a jutting lamp-oil tank,
a gorse face fans out,
its sheaves fought over by gulls.

Our place of recovery
is a place of monks and salted chocolate;
of air clicking in the ash trees.

We comb the cliff edge
each of us singled out by the wind.
We are gulped down by it.

On the horizon
we spot a mass of clouds hissing;
so we head back to the boat,

which returns us to dry land
just as rain
fills countless holiday-home backyards.

SHAKESPEARE INSULT KIT

Soothe then this memory
of sons at breakfast;
their brutal, betrothing
nature turned loose.

Hawk sky hangs
between here and the clouds.
It is the hanger of clouds
being itself disentangled.

We may well
return to this point
in another lifetime
or maybe two.

Or maybe there will be
no returning at all.
Cheat, lie, steal; bring
disrepute into disrepute.

Bang on the floor
with as hollow a knock
as can be mustered
by any action.

Only the remit of now
has any sense to it.
Me here now,
what else?

It sounds like the girls
are getting up
with their more genuine reflections
on the way life is.

A houseful groans
at the thought of growing up.
Peace returns
over toast.

CHANGING ROOM

Grey-brown tiles grid mildly
through layers of steam.

Even as vents ease water from the air
ceiling squares flood and rot.

Through a grille a wire curls upwards
joining a spar in part-shadow.

Shapely benches line up
on rust spots left by old bolts.

Cocks are massaged as men shower
in light diffused by soap.

Everywhere mirrors blaze,
pretty with raised blood.

In the frame, a cheeky pin-fine
tattoo lies hurdled over muscle.

In Japan, the giving of a flayed tattoo
as an heirloom continues.

HE IS TO BE HERE

'They remained standing, and those lie in an [underground] plot who once ruled the earth, who owned its hearths, who had nobody near them…from now on only the god Inshushinak speaks his commands forever in the grave.'
Elamite Prayer

Cut flowers reflect on stone;
parallel lit stalks
dipped in water.

So it's here:
A field for the horror faces
to bow under.

Whatever there is in finished matter
will be sustained, perhaps,
by channels of wine,

allowing the newly planted to grow like this,
spread underground amongst seeds
of copper and iron.

Action here always is less than it should be.
Stems sabre vases,
but refuse to ignite;

fingers done with fighting grow loose,
suffering a difference
of more than just degree.

Yet here they remain as dry,
simultaneous matter.
Bones' big empty spaces sustained in full,

needed like drink;
as they listen to the stark
slaughter-music of the high distant hills.

FLOE

Winter body
returning
returning
to the cold
it belongs to.
Arctic organ.
Frost limb.
Pity lost in a constant
whiteout
preventing
vision.

Winter body;
snow-tongued,
crack-lipped,
lapping at the cool sea.
Melting
when the seasonal thaw
takes hold.
Return
return
the bare rock
of a lost continent.

ESPECIAL DISSOLUTION

I

I wake
under the sign of Corvus.

I scratch my eyes;
I stretch out in the conservatory;
I sit in the scaled cold.

Relaxing is definitely easier when a chain of being
has tacked plants and animals and cars
to a world above the clouds.

There's an attack up in the trees,
I can't see it,
but I can hear a kraahing
followed by a rattle,
followed by a kraahing again.

Maybe they're ancestors
                fighting over a bowl of water;
maybe they're ancestors
                gathering in a ghost-tree.

I imagine their posturing, black-fingered wings;
the head bobbing, the dipping, the grieving beaks.

I imagine the kraah becoming the Vaak;
pressing itself into a universe that moves through my pores
like dust through an opened window;
like the slick leech-creep of pure spirit
oozing up the brick-work to perch on a roof top
like a drawn tooth.

There's more calling. I should feed them really.

How about a bowl of beer?

Yes, surf-topped,
beautiful as the sun;
full of the sun which streams down
to create good aurorae and good beer.

There was a coronal mass ejection that year -
a beautiful coronal stream in fact
that collided with our magnetic field
to produce some very intense flavours.

Hmmm..
          yes, how about going to the pub?

II

So, what am I doing?

Well, I'm waking up; I'm holding a drum;
I'm shouting at my son in a car park;
I'm holding fire;
I'm deciding over breakfast;
I'm hearing rain;
I'm waking up;
I'm waking up;
I'm waking

I'm...
'I'm dancing with a bird in a nightclub,
it's got tits and blonde hair and a cock like a snake.
I have sex with it,
but does that make me gay?'

The barber snips a bit more hair.
'One of my older customers said he didn't regret doing that years ago.
He could have not done it, but he did,
and then he was much happier.
The rich cunt.'

A hen-do passes, pissed up on the street.

Unsure how to draw out the conversation
the barber pauses,
'So, sex with a pre-op transsexual -
gay sex or not gay sex?'

More hair than I can spare hits the floor.
I answer like a tooth-drawer:
'All things will dissolve then resolve eventually –
It might matter. It might not.'

More snipping.
'But when that 8-inch sword is wagging in your face,
                                              it matters.'

Ah the decision tree,
rattling with warish sparrows.

Now I'm awake.
Now I'm awake and back on the serpent, holding fire;
in fact I'm holding the fierce fire of the sun.

III

Other universes sketch their presences in the margins.
Golden, womb-ended stump universes;
abortion-yanked, yowl-clanked multiverses
burping in the pre-dark.
They are unable to will themselves into life quite yet;
they're just waiting for the bulb pop that will let them in;
just waiting for a god to wake them up.

And no-one will remember what went before.
And no-one will be able to think about what might come after.
This might be all after all, or this might be nothing.

So then, let's be off to the pub in the rain to consider our options.

There isn't a fire, so we have to sit at the bar with the masticating general
public;
luckily the beer and the wine dopes us nicely as these fuckers come in:
Short fuckers; jeans-with-zips fuckers;
smug vinegar-tongued mother fuckers
who've remembered to put their kids in waterproofs.

Ooh, these twats know their limits;
decision-happy with half-a-glass of port.
I mean, I am a twatty bastard myself,
but half-a-glass of port, really?
And then no doubt it'll be off to Venice
to enjoy the sand with the kids but completely ignore the light.

The world is theirs though, I suppose.

Something else was going on in that parallel world however.
In each gut a taught, cellular machinery was working overtime.
Feeding it can make it overproduce in a way that creates the ageing process.
So, I enjoy watching these tits, eating themselves old.

Then I remember that I'm filling my guts too
with hops, malt, sugar, barley, preservatives, peanuts.

So what should I do? Drink or not drink?

That fucking decision tree.

Well, I might play bar skittles, or I might play pocket billiards;
I might go and clip my toe nails;
I am most certainly not going back to fix a fucking fence.

I might be all,
        I might be nothing.
              I'm waking up.

IV

Sister Aimee Semple Macpherson returns
from her kidnap to an ordeal of petals
dropped by robed angelic girls
and a low fly-by of planes.

Still sore from the desert;
still sore from that caboose-shaped
dent in her hotel bed. Still sore from the logic
of that hell-born bastard theory.

Sister Aimee, why did you try?
With that hot hot-potato ass,
why worry about a house
where The Lord is or isn't?

When the bacillus dropped you, what angels came then?
Or did death just stand cock-upright with an arrow and an hourglass?
I will rescue you from that if you want -
maybe I've rescued you already.

V

(i)   Speaking of which, me,
a Historian and a Geographer
are in a boozer.

We'd been on the continental lagers
which came in big cylindrical glasses.
We were talking to a local

who was discussing stolen relics
in a pissed-up, over-the-rainbow lingo
even the Historian couldn't understand.

Then Time herself turned up,
hammered and spouting off:
'3 of my boys: 41, 43 and 45 -

or some combination like that.
How long have I given you?
5 more meetings perhaps... 10?

That sounds too generous you say?
Hmm, I am a bitch of a giver though,
always demanding as I offer you my hand..

Still, 10 it is if you're lucky.
It's only maths anyway lads,
drab little numbers.

And you can imagine 10
as clear as well-water;
and you can picture that seeping away.

(ii) What is also clear
is that you doubt even my existence -
I am, apparently, merely a function of your brains.
Well, maybe, but then, perhaps I transcend everything.
Maybe I've presided over universes before.
Dirty universes, gutted universes.

Maybe this isn't the first and maybe it won't be the last;
just the latest using heat from the last,
preparing to pass heat on to the next,
in a distorting, detectable cycle -
an endless sequence of cycles in fact.
Delectable, detectable sequences of cycles.

(iii)   Ah lovely,

three golden cylinders,

a round for my boys.

Drink, drink!

This is why you were born.

Drink! Drink!

Because this is your task.

By drinking

you will know.

By drinking

you will know

of all the traditions of your fathers.

By drinking,

you will be brave.

I will help you...

Waken boys.

Waken boys.

Wake to joy.'

(iv)   At that point Time staggered off
to chat to the pissed up cunt
standing at a central pier
dangling from the roof.
Then the Geographer had to go
because his wife came to pick him up.
It was all a shame really,
because we'd just gotten through
to piecing that rolling, bar-world together:
the roof as the sky;
brilliant fake mineral pillars as the mountains;
the floor-space as the earth;
and beneath that the nether world
of plastered bones and shells
stuck into eye-sockets
to act as constant
watchers over
the living.
Shiny,
odd
balls

(v) Still, that left me with the Historian,
so we trundled off to a kebab shop,
got chips and wound up drinking real ale
in as late a bar as the town offered.
We discussed an Iron Age golden cape and it's ritualistic role.
Then we discussed the breeding habits of the Red Kite.

(vi) When we finally strolled home
we took in a local crystal meth factory
that had used a council house as its base.

VI

Unreal?
How about unethereal?
Yes; unethereal.

So, unethereal town.
No. Unethereal, pointless town.
No. Unethereal, pointless town, whose inhabitants call it 'SCreweD'?

Yes.
Unethereal
pointless
Screwed
town.

Yes. Unethereal, unreal, unsealed
unrhythmic, chav-mythic
bong-chonging, no-one-belonging
six-toed, brought-down, too-real town.

Anyway, since I'm looking at the place I suppose I'd better write this:

UNDER THE SIGN OF CORVUS

Three back windows shine
On the walls of two houses
Whose blacknesses I know.

Everything I see from this point
Is filtered through the side-flap
Of a plastic-walled growhouse.

It shines too; somber fighter
Against the dark.
I'm grateful it's light is there.

Night air comes in and cools me;
I think how the dead need tending
Just like plants do.

Unscrewing a bulb before bed I look again,
But then there were just shades,
Dark against a more frenzied dark.

Hmm... trying shit.

This might matter, it might not.
It almost certainly won't.
It's been written before
and better.

However, I am a venal, bitch-boned, cock-sucker
and I'm desperate enough to try nursery rhymes
and foreign languages, perhaps Polish.

No, no to rhymes, no to Polish.

Oh, hang on...

Blotnisty kopyta, blotniste kopyta
w ciemnosci pod dachami
Co moze sie zdarzyc w lesie?
Smierc lub zycie
Siedzi na noz.

See, it's a bit gowno isn't it?

But then again, much cleverer,
more sensitive men,
they try harder don't they?

And...
       ...sorry, I'm being a tosser
and not in the best sense of that word.

It's all been said before;
said better and more clearly.

By better men.

VII

a) Even so it was death that stamped its feet first,
as poor old Mr H. Jones stood on a path
of old till and mudstone
birthing a tornado.

His wife had died and by his hedge
he and my dad talked while I stood,
quietly noticing his eyes
subsiding to the deepest limit of their sockets.

Our curtains were closed all that week
and I think I remember the hearse,
but I could be making that up.

Not long after we made the street close its curtains
and I think, though I'm not sure, Mr H. Jones saw my dad
and held his elbow and held him with his words.
But he also held him with his eyes:
slits still; loess-yellowish-grey; utterly sunken.

There was no language there but that of the ground:
Breccia, siltstone, evaporite, coal, shit.
All of it offering a mineral-salted water-comfort
to be trapped in hollow eye-ducts.

b) Then I remember.

The drum starts and then I remember laughing
in Mr H. Jones' garden at a party.

I remember loudness and running.
I remember Mrs H. Jones.

I remember Mrs H. Jones

I remember, I remember,
I remember crows claws rattling on the conservatory roof.

I remember the drum of their wings.

I remember waking up to a bright day
after a day spent drinking with people above-ground.

I remember a sun's fire, the Sun's fire-path.

I remember waking up.
I remember drum-wings banging and then waking up.

I remember drum-wings and a serpent-seething cold;
I remember waking to a universe teething.

And that might have been all: And that might have been nothing.

I was awake;
I remember I was awake.

I remember waking up.
            Waking up.
                    Wake up.
                            Wake.